A man in a passion rides a mad horse.

The year 2006 marked the 300th birthday of one of America's greatest contributors to civilization: Benjamin Franklin. Among other things, Franklin was a founding father, scientist, philosopher, businessman, inventor, statesman, author, and printer. His many accomplishments were largely the result of persistence and hard work—virtues that are the subject of many of the proverbs Franklin gave to the world in the 1700s. For 25 years, he espoused these morals in his famous publication Poor Richard's Almanack.

While books were scarce in the American colonies, most people had two—a Bible and an Almanack. Franklin did not author all of the proverbs he published; many had already been in use for years before he wrote them down. But what he did do was spread these sayings throughout the colonies in hopes that they would promote upright living and a hardworking society—a society that would become united in purpose as well as in name: the United States of America.

Michael McCurdy

Designed by Rita Marshall

SO
SAID
BEN

DRAWINGS BY MICHAEL McCURDY

CREATIVE EDITIONS

Mankato, Minnesota

To lengthen thy life, lessen thy meals.

While living and working with his older brother James as a teenager, Ben felt a stronger hunger for books than for the food James fed him. So the two struck a deal. Ben would eat cheaply on bread, fruit, vegetables, and water. The rest of his food money could be spent on books. Ben ate this healthy diet for the rest of his life, living to age 84.

He that lieth down with dogs shall rise up with fleas.

Ben believed in avoiding bad company and surrounding himself with people who had a positive influence on his life. His wife Deborah was a kind woman who gave Ben friendship and support. When he worked as a printer, she often worked by his side. He also made friends with many important thinkers, artists, politicians, and writers who wanted to do good things for the world.

They that won't be counseled can't be helped.

As a diplomat, Ben listened carefully to the Americans he represented. In England, he tried to explain why the American colonies should have freedom from Britain. The British didn't want to hear what Ben had to say. He tried to help the British see what was coming, but their stubbornness wouldn't allow it. The American colonies soon declared war.

Every man thinks his own geese swans.

In Ben's case, turkeys were swans. He wanted the wild turkey to be the symbol for America. In his opinion, eagles were lazy because they stole the prey of other birds. But turkeys were respectable. Ben had high standards and upheld traits that he admired. He tried to be humble, but he often thought that his opinions were the best!

A lie stands on one leg, the truth on two.

Ben learned the importance of honesty early in life. As a young boy, he often played at a nearby pond, fishing, swimming, and sailing. One day, he and some friends made a dock using stones that were to be used to build a house. When Ben's father learned what the boys had done, he demanded that Ben return the stones, saying "that which is not honest cannot truly be useful."

Little strokes fell great oaks.

Ben believed that people could achieve almost anything through hard work. Success, in his mind, never happened overnight. He worked as a printer until he owned his own printing press. He also did many experiments to develop the lightning rod and bifocal eyeglasses. One of the founding fathers of the United States, Ben reached that position by starting as a local Pennsylvania politician.

Early to bed, early to rise, makes a man healthy, wealthy, and wise.

Throughout his life, Ben understood the importance of image. He knew that people often put more trust in a person who was up early in the day and appeared busy. So Ben used his time carefully. He tried to keep a strict schedule for work, dining, music, conversation, thought, and sleep. He was usually awake at five A.M. and in bed by nine P.M.

A penny saved is a penny earned.

Ben came from a poor family but learned early on to work hard and save his money. He didn't buy unnecessary items like fancy clothes or powdered wigs (which most men wore at the time). He often dressed simply, in a plain brown suit and a fur cap. In 1928, the United States began using Ben's face to decorate the $100 bill.

The doors of wisdom are never shut.

Ben attended school for only two years of his life, but he never stopped learning. He educated himself by reading everything that passed before his eyes. He was curious and intelligent, but he knew that he needed to study hard and learn from his experiences. Although he worked long hours at his various jobs, he always made time for reading and reflection.

Speak little, do much.

In his lifetime, Ben accomplished far more than most people ever dream of. He was a printer, a scientist, an inventor, a politician, and a diplomat—and was a rousing success at each job. In his opinion, dwelling on the past or dreaming about the future was simply a waste of time. Less was accomplished whenever people's mouths moved and their hands stayed still.

Tart words make no friends: a spoonful of honey will catch more flies than a gallon of vinegar.

Ben was not a very smooth public speaker, but he had a talent for talking with people one-on-one and putting them at ease. Being considerate and kind in small ways—remembering someone's name or listening to his problems—earned him many friends. Ben knew that he didn't need nice clothes or money to impress people. Being himself and showing an interest in others was much more effective.

He who falls in love with himself will have no rivals.

While living in France, Ben became a superstar of sorts. The French admired his simple manner and charm, and they began putting his picture on everything—including watches, rings, and medallions. Ben tried not to let this attention go to his head. He believed that focusing on oneself too much could ruin a person's understanding of the world. Being humble was very important.

If you would not be forgotten as soon as you are dead and rotten, either write things worth reading or do things worth the writing.

During his lifetime, Ben became well known for his actions and his words. He tried to live as an example of honesty, and this helped him make lasting friendships throughout the world. He helped to write the Declaration of Independence and the Constitution of the United States. Today he is remembered as one of America's founding fathers and wisest citizens.

Benjamin Franklin was born in Boston, Massachusetts, in 1706. He was the eighth child of ten born into a strict Puritan family. His father worked hard as a candle maker, but it was difficult for the family to rise out of poverty. Because of this, Ben attended school for only two years. He always loved reading, however, and his desire to learn—through books and hands-on experiences—followed him throughout his life.

At age 12, Ben became an apprentice at his older brother James's printing press, reading everything that came through the shop. Soon, he began writing his own opinions about Boston politics and society under the pen name "Mrs. Silence Dogood." The brothers often argued, and at age 17, Ben broke his apprenticeship agreement and ran away, finding work at a printing press in Philadelphia. He eventually bought his own press and, over the next two decades, became well known for his printing and editing work throughout the New England colonies.

During his time as a printer, Ben began working on Poor Richard's Almanack, a book in which he shared his beliefs in hard work, thrift, and honesty. He also spent his time improving the quality of life in Philadelphia. Because books were scarce in the colonies, he organized the first subscription library, allowing people to borrow books for a small fee. He also rallied support for public programs to clean up, pave, and light Philadelphia's streets.

Around this same time, Ben began testing his practical ideas about science. He invented swim fins, bifocals, a musical instrument called the glass armonica, and the Franklin stove, a stove that used little wood but produced much heat. He did experiments to prove that lightning was a kind of electricity and created the lightning rod. The device became a noticeable addition to buildings throughout the colonies, as it could save them from fire by routing lightning harmlessly into the ground.

By living frugally, Ben made enough money to retire from his printing career at age 42. He would not be satisfied, however, with a life of leisure. Only three years later, in 1751, Ben was elected to the Pennsylvania Assembly, a government position that allowed him to help shape the laws of the American colonies. His career in government spanned the next 40 years.

From 1757 to 1762, Ben worked as a diplomat to England, sharing ideas about the American colonies. In his early days in England, he fell in love with British culture and intellectual society. Blinded by this love, he thought that America would benefit if it stayed under the control of England. But he listened carefully to the frustrations of the American colonists and, in time, realized that the colonies would flourish if they were independent. He helped draft the Declaration of Independence and was among those who immediately signed it.

Ben also kindled a lasting friendship with the French people, serving as a diplomat to their country from 1776 to 1785. In France, he gained military support for America's war of independence from Britain by making behind-the-scenes connections with French officials. He returned to America a hero.

In the last five years of his life, Ben served as the president (top government official) of Pennsylvania, worked to abolish slavery throughout the colonies, and participated in the writing and ratifying of the Constitution of the United States. He died in 1790 at age 84. While more than 20,000 people attended his funeral in Pennsylvania, millions more throughout America and France mourned his loss.

In 1976, a marble statue of Ben was erected in Philadelphia in memory of the city's most famous son and one of America's best-loved founding fathers. Three centuries after his birth, he is still remembered for his vast wisdom.

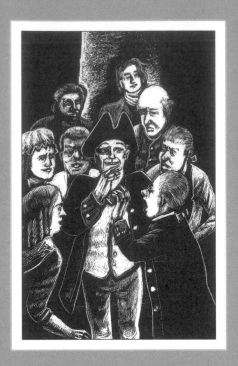

Drawings copyright © 2007 Michael McCurdy

Published in 2007 by Creative Editions

P.O. Box 227, Mankato, MN 56002 USA

Creative Editions is an imprint of The Creative Company.

Designed by Rita Marshall

Edited by Aaron Frisch

Printed in Italy

Library of Congress Cataloging-in-Publication Data

McCurdy, Michael. So said Ben / by Michael McCurdy.

ISBN: 978-1-56846-147-2

1. Franklin, Benjamin, 1706–1790–Juvenile literature.

2. Franklin, Benjamin, 1706–1790–Quotations–Juvenile literature.

3. Statesmen–United States–Biography–Juvenile literature.

4. Scientists–United States–Biography–Juvenile literature.

5. Inventors–United States–Biography–Juvenile literature.

6. Printers–United States–Biography–Juvenile literature. I. Title.

E302.6.F8M125 2007   973.3092–dc22 [B]   2006027667

First edition

2 4 6 8 9 7 5 3 1